VIET CONG
A Photographic Portrait

Edward J. Emering

Schiffer Military History
Atglen, PA

Hello new friend
we meet
and you are dead
all you'll ever know of me
is copper jacket lead

On six old bucks
two meals a day
over half the earth I came
to kill you
who never saw my face
and never knew my name.

Ned Broderick
Chicago, Illinois

"If you hold a real weapon in your hand, you will feel its character strongly. It begs to be used. It is fearsome. Its only purpose is death, and its power is not just in the material from which it is made, but also from the intention of its makers.

It is regrettable that weapons must sometimes be used, but occasionally, survival demands it. The wise go forth with weapons only as a last resort. They never rejoice in the skill of weapons, nor do they glorify war.

When death, pain and destruction are visited upon what you hold to be most sacred, the spiritual price is devastating. What hurts more than one's own suffering is bearing witness to the suffering of others. The regret of seeing human beings at their worst and the sheer pain of not being able to help the victims can never be redeemed.

If you go personally to war, you cross the line yourself. You sacrifice ideals for survival and the fury of killing. That alters you forever. That is why no one rushes to be a soldier. Think before you want to change so unalterably. The stakes are not merely one's life, but one's very humanity."

Thoughts on War
Deng Ming-Dao, a Taoist monk
Several thousand years before Christ

Dedication:

To Commander Frank C. Brown, M.D., USN (1948-1998), warrior, hero, healer, author, adventurer, collector and friend. Your legacy will live on in the hearts of those who were privileged to have known you.

Acknowledgments:

Grateful thanks to the National Vietnam Veterans Art Museum, Chicago, Illinois, for allowing me access to the Frank C. Brown Photographic Collection and other ancillary artifacts and materials. Thanks also to my good friends, Ned Broderick, for allowing me to include his poem, and Gerry Schooler, for the photo of Vo Bam.

Book Design by Ian Robertson.

Copyright © 1999 by Edward J. Emering.
Library of Congress Catalog Number: 98-88556

Printed in China.
ISBN: 0-7643-0758-4

We are interested in hearing from authors with book ideas on related topics.

Published by Schiffer Publishing Ltd.
4880 Lower Valley Road
Atglen, PA 19310
Phone: (610) 593-1777
FAX: (610) 593-2002
E-mail: Schifferbk@aol.com.
Visit our web site at: www.schifferbooks.com
Please write for a free catalog.
This book may be purchased from the publisher.
Please include $3.95 postage.
Try your bookstore first.

In Europe, Schiffer books are distributed by:
Bushwood Books
6 Marksbury Road
Kew Gardens
Surrey TW9 4JF
England
Phone: 44 (0)181 392-8585
FAX: 44 (0)181 392-9876
E-mail: Bushwd@aol.com.

Try your bookstore first.

CONTENTS

PREFACE

Ed Emering has long been dedicated to developing and promoting the artifact collection and research materials of the National Vietnam Veterans Art Museum in Chicago, Illinois. The Museum, which is based upon the collective works of more than 100 international (including North Vietnamese and Viet Cong) artists, sculptors, and photographers, who served in the Vietnam War (1960-1975), moved into its permanent facility in August 1996. A great deal of thanks is due to the City of Chicago and Mayor and Mrs. Richard M. Daley for their support and assistance in establishing a permanent home for this national treasure.

With the advent of a permanent site to house the Museum's growing art collection, attention has been turned toward adding artifacts and research materials. The Museum recently acquired two significant photo collections. The first details the efforts and experiences of the Royal Australian Regiment (RAR) in Phuoc Tuy Province, III Corps, and was graciously made available by the Australian War Memorial Museum in Canberra. The second, a private collection of more than 1,200 captured Viet Cong photographs, has served as the inspiration and basis for this work.

Two of Ed's previous works (see Bibliography) have dealt with the orders and decorations of the enemy and the weapons and field gear of the enemy, and have established his expertise on such matters. In 1997 and 1998 he was awarded Literary Medals by the Orders and Medals Society of America (OMSA) for his numerous articles on NVA and Viet Cong decorations, which have been featured in the *The Medal Collector*, the Journal of OMSA. Much of his information has been gathered from the study of enemy photographs. The latest photo collection acquisitions will serve to broaden and deepen such insights.

I believe that this work will provide significant new insights into the Viet Cong for the reader, while the photographs will become a valuable source for future researchers and authors.

B. B. T. Langtree
Historian
Chicago, Illinois

INTRODUCTION

I am no stranger to the enemy, nor did I know him. Who was he really? Was he violent? Was he a master of terrorism? Was he an evil menace? Was he lonely and frightened? Many Vietnam veterans can pose this question—most cannot answer it. I would not be so presumptuous to assume that I could, either. Of course, the Viet Cong were all these things and more, but as the artist, Ned Broderick, points out in his very poignant poem, to most, the enemy was merely a stranger. I would, therefore, encourage readers to look closely and to draw his or her own conclusions about the enemy. I think that such conclusions will vary widely.

The political climate in Vietnam, which gave rise to the National Liberation Front (NLF, or Viet Cong), was complex and often inscrutable. The division of the nation at the 17th Parallel at the Geneva Peace Conference in 1954 led to the eventual evolvement of the Diem regime in South Vietnam. Ngo Dinh Diem and his relatives pursued a troubling and repressive political course, which gave rise to many internal opposition groups in the late 50s. It was this troubling course which eventually led the U.S. to lend its support to a bloody coup in 1963, resulting in the deaths of Diem and his brother, Nhu, head of South Vietnam's Secret Police. By then, however, it was too late. The communist opposition, or Viet Cong, had carefully and cleverly structured the NLF to embrace the various disenfranchised groups within South Vietnam. These included more than 20 diverse organizations, whose common bond was suffering at the hands of the Diem regime.

In due course, this political opposition escalated into armed opposition against the South Vietnamese government, secretly supported at first (and, subsequently, openly supported) by the Communist Party and government of North Vietnam. This armed opposition was initially carried out by lightly equipped guerrilla bands. In some cases, these were part time warriors; in others, full time armed opposition groups were established. These guerrilla soldiers, both male and female, are often seen in the classic black pajama garb of the peasant class. Their weapons were usually basic carbine rifles, in some cases homemade.

These guerrilla groups were eventually supplemented by professional Liberation Army units, recruited locally, but often led by southerners trained in North Vietnam and infiltrated into South Vietnam along the Ho Chi Minh Trail. Their uniforms, although absent of any rank insignia, were more formal in nature. Their weapons and equipment were also far more sophisticated, including assault rifles, light and heavy machine guns, mortars, and portable rocket launchers.

In this, my fourth book for Schiffer Publishing, I was fortunate to be able to avail myself of a captured Viet Cong photo collection acquired on behalf of the National Vietnam Veterans Art Museum from U.S. Navy Commander Frank

C. Brown. I felt that publication of these photographs would help to place a face on the enemy and to define the Viet Cong in more human terms.

Most of the photos contained in this work were taken in III Corps, which was comprised of the Provinces of Tay Ninh, the sight of some of the bloodiest encounters between the Viet Cong 5 and 7 Divisions and the U.S. Army's 1st Air Cavalry Division and 25th Division, Binh Long, Phuoc Long, Long Khanh, Binh Tuy, Phuoc Tuy, an area of heavy encounters between the Viet Cong 5 Division and the Australian Royal Army Regiment (RAR), Bien Hoa, home to a major U.S. air base and numerous Viet Cong encounters, Binh Duong, Hau Nghia, and Long An.

As Mark Moyer indicates in his book, *Phoenix and Other Birds of Prey*, photographs were a cultural obsession among the Vietnamese. The Viet Cong had their photographs taken regularly, even at remote jungle bases. These photographs were often captured at hastily abandoned enemy jungle camps or taken from the packs of slain Viet Cong guerrillas. It would not be unusual for a soldier to be carrying a photograph of himself and several members of his squad posing with weapons or a NLF flag.

Large collections of these photographs were amassed by numerous Allied organizations, including the South Vietnamese Secret Police and the Provincial Reconnaissance Units (PRUs), the enforcement branch of the Phuong Hoang, or Phoenix Program. Captured photos were matched with the faces of villagers in an effort to identify them as Viet Cong. In a number of instances, the photographs included in this work are marked with an "X." It has been assumed that this indicates an identification of that particular person had been made. In other cases, photographs of leading Viet Cong political and military figures were readily available. Certainly, NLF President Tho, Vice Commander of the NLF Madame Dinh, and the lovely, but deadly, Hero of the Liberation Army, Myoi Li (known as Ta Thi Kieu) were examples of well known and frequently photographed Viet Cong personalities.

It is with this background that I share representative selections from this highly valued collection with the reader. Whether your interest lies in collecting medals or field gear, or just simply a desire to view candid photographs of the enemy, I am sure you will find it interesting. In a limited number of instances individuals depicted in the photographs have been identified. Both myself and the staff of the National Vietnam Veterans Art Museum would be interested in hearing from others who might be able to contribute to the identification of the captured photographs presented herein.

Edward J. Emering
Chicago, Illinois

A BRIEF HISTORY OF THE
NATIONAL LIBERATION FRONT (VIET CONG)

No sooner had the First Indochina War ended with the bitter defeat of the French Colonial Army at Dien Bien Phu on May 8, 1954, than the seeds for further discontent were sown at Geneva, Switzerland. The Geneva Peace Conference, chaired jointly by Great Britain and the Soviet Union, resulted in the temporary partition of Vietnam at the 17th Parallel. The State of South Vietnam would be led by Emperor Bao Dai (1913-1997). In June, 1954, he chose as his Prime Minister Ngo Dinh Diem (1901-1963). Diem, a Catholic, had been born into a high Mandarin family, serving at the imperial court in Hue. Educated in France and the United States, Diem ascended to the role of Prime Minister with a reputation as a strong anti-communist and anti-colonialist. Diem soon revealed a disposition toward nepotism and favoritism, appointing many relatives and Catholics to significant posts in the new government.

Diem dethroned Bao Dai in 1955, and in October declared the establishment of the Republic of Vietnam, appointing himself as its new President. His brother Ngo Dinh Nhu (1910-1963) headed the powerful secret police. His brother's wife Tran Le Xuan (Madame Nhu) (1924-), known to Americans as the Dragon Lady, headed the anti-communist paramilitary organization known as the Vietnamese Women's Solidarity Movement. More importantly, she used her intellect and energy to exert significant influence on both her bachelor brother-in-law, Diem, and her husband, Nhu. She was referred to as, "the woman who ruled the men who ruled Vietnam." Her caustic cynicism, freely expressed in public statements, would cause widespread rancor both at home and abroad, especially in Washington.

It was Diem's next moves that caused far reaching discontent and disenfranchisement in the South. He aggressively pursued repressive campaigns against all potential opposition. His first target was the armed paramilitary forces of the Binh Xuyen, the Cao Dai, and the Hoa Hao.

The Binh Xuyen was in effect Saigon's mafia. Formed by a fusion of bandit gangs under the leadership of Bay Vien, the Binh Xuyen grew into a well disciplined paramilitary organization, numbering more than 40,000 soldiers. The Cao Dai and Hoa Hao were religious sects, each of which maintained its own armed forces. The Cao Dai favored political factions opposed to Diem. They joined with the armed Buddhist sect, Hoa Hao, and the Binh Xuyen to resist Diem. Diem's brother Nhu took personal responsibility for defeating the combined Binh Xuyen, Cao Dai and Hoa Hao armies.

Once accomplished, Diem turned his focus to the Communists, dubbed Viet Nam Cong San, or Viet Cong. The South Vietnamese Communist Party strongly opposed Diem's often brutal attempts at subverting earlier land reform measures, implemented following the Viet Minh's victory over the French Colonial Forces. Diem's government often returned land parcels previously ceded to peasants by the Viet Minh to their former owners. The Diem government added injury to insult by awarding back rent payments to the original owners.

By the fall of 1957, the Communist Party had turned to armed opposition to the Diem regime. The Party, which had heretofore followed political dau tranh (struggle), now turned to armed dau tranh. Although not many recognized it at the time, the Second Indochina War had begun. Early armed opposition efforts were carried out by local guerrilla forces. These were generally part time militia squads, which were often poorly armed and equipped. In many cases, they made use of antiquated (WWI) or homemade weapons. They typically operated in and around specific villages, attacking small, rural government offices and installations at night and returning to their families and land during the day, giving rise to the saying "Farmers by day, warriors at night."

Observing this unrest, the Politburo (ruling body) in Hanoi decided to lend material support. On May 9, 1959, they authorized formation of the top secret Group 559, also known as the 559th Transportation Company. This Group, under then Major (subsequently Major General) Vo Bam, would establish and operate the Truong Son Route, which would become known to the world as the Ho Chi Minh Trail. Initially, it was decided to funnel captured French and even WWII Japanese, German, and U.S. weapons into the South in support of local guerrilla activities to disguise the actual source of support for the Southern communists. The weapons furnished included carbines, submachine guns and light machine guns. The Trail would eventually be supported by the Truong Son Command, consisting of more than 100,000 personnel, which would move more than 20,000 PAVN regular forces and tons of supplies and equipment into the South every month.

During July, 1959, 4,000 southerners, who had moved from the South to the North in the fall of 1954, following the partition of their country, began infiltrating into South Vietnam along the arduous Ho Chi Minh Trail. Although they encountered a certain level of resentment in some quarters, they helped local guerrillas estab-

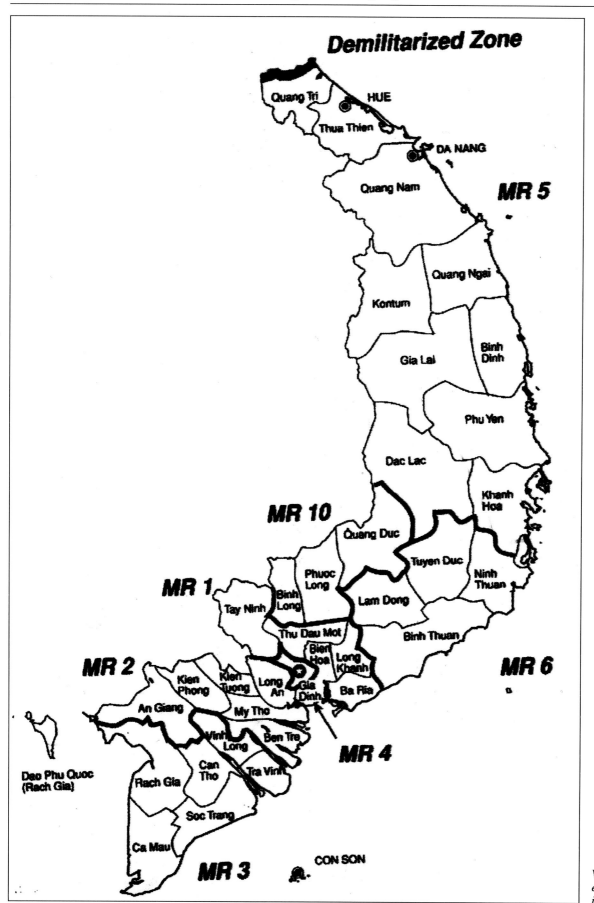

Demilitarized Zone

Quang Tri

HUE

Thua Thien

DA NANG

Quang Nam

MR 5

Quang Ngai

Kontum

Binh Dinh

Gia Lai

Phu Yen

Dac Lac

Khanh Hoa

MR 10

Quang Duc

Tuyen Duc

Ninh Thuan

MR 1

Phuoc Long

Binh Long

Tay Ninh

Lam Dong

Thu Dau Mot

Binh Thuan

Bien Hoa

Long Khanh

MR 6

MR 2

Kien Phong

Kien Tuong

Long An

Gia Dinh

Ba Ria

An Giang

My Tho

Ben Tre

Vinh Long

MR 4

Dao Phu Quoc (Rach Gia)

Can Tho

Tra Vinh

Rach Gia

Soc Trang

Ca Mau

MR 3

CON SON

Viet Cong military operational regions (MR) in South Vietnam.

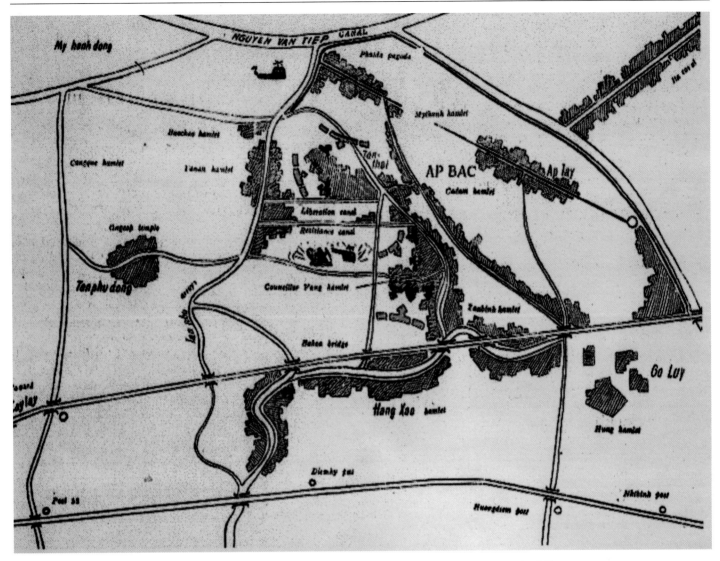

Viet Cong map taken from captured booklet detailing ambushes (arrows) at the battle of Ap Bac on January 2, 1963.

lish strongholds in the Mekong Delta, Central Highlands and Coastal Plains regions. It was these "regroupees" who helped shape and lead the full time guerrilla units operating at the Provincial and District levels. They would in time form the nucleus of the more heavily equipped "main force" Viet Cong army units.

On December 31, 1960, the National Liberation Front (Mat Tran Dan Toc Giai Phong Mien Nam) was formed. Its stated objectives included: national independence, social justice, and democratic reforms. The NLF was outwardly postured as an umbrella organization for all disenfranchised groups in South Vietnam. In this guise, the NLF attracted support from more than 20 diverse oppressed groups in South Vietnam. In reality, the NLF was the spawn of the Vietnamese (Communist) Workers' Party (Dang Lao Dong Vietnam). These links to the Communist Party in North Vietnam were kept a closely guarded secret.

Nguyen Huu Tho (1910-1996), a radical lawyer who had been prominently involved in the Saigon peace movement and subsequently imprisoned in 1955 by the Diem regime in South Vietnam, was elected President of the NLF. He was chosen for his broad

appeal, but was primarily a figurehead for his entire tenure (1960-1976). Other leading members of the NLF's Central Committee included: Huyen Tan Phat, an architect; Nguyen Van Hieu, a teacher; Tran Buu Kiem, a Communist Party member and one of the original organizers of the NLF; Ung Ngoc Ky, a teacher; and Truong Nhu Trang, an attorney. Primary representatives included: Pram Xuan Thai (youth); Nguyen Huu The (peasants); Nguyen Co Tam (workers); Nguyen Thi Dinh (1920-1992) (women); and General Tran Nam Trung, commander-in-chief of the People's Liberation Armed Forces (PLAF) and COSVN (see below) member. Madame Dinh also served as vice commander of the PLAF. This was the highest ranking PLAF position held by a woman (although some commentators have described her position as ceremonial). She, along with President Tho, were highly visible in photographs taken at the NLF's political/propaganda gatherings.

With the formation of the NLF at the end of 1960, the ground work was laid for the emergence of a true liberation army. This army would have a more formal structure supplanting the work done by the part time and full time guerrilla units. The People's

Ap Bac medal.

Liberation Armed Force (PLAF) was formally established on February 15, 1961. It adopted as the NLF flag, a vertically divided red (top) and blue (bottom) background with a gold star. Beginning in 1963, the NLF introduced its own system of orders and decorations to recognize and reward outstanding achievement. In time, some of these orders and decorations became official awards of the unified country.

In reality, the PLAF operated as an extension of North Vietnam's People's Army of Vietnam (PAVN) under direct control of the Central Committee Directorate for the South, referred to as the Central Office for South Vietnam, or COSVN, by the Allies. The PLAF had its own military leadership, originally under Lieutenant General Tran Nam Trung, as part of the effort to maintain its disguise of independence (from Hanoi). In reality, its activities were ultimately coordinated by PAVN military leaders. Initially, the PLAF competed with the Army of the Republic of Vietnam (ARVN) for local recruits, including women, ethnic Cambodians, and Montagnards (members of the 33 various mountain tribes who inhabited the southern half of the Annamite mountain range). In its formative stages, the PLAF also relied heavily on those southerners who had been infiltrated into South Vietnam along the Ho Chi Minh Trail. With the reemergence of the Regional Forces/Popular Forces in South Vietnam at the village level, the Viet Cong were eventually denied a critically important source of local recruits. Greater and greater reliance had to be placed on PAVN forces being infiltrated into the South along the Ho Chi Minh Trail. In 1964, PAVN Senior General Nguyen Chi Thanh (1914-1967) assumed control of COSVN and the overall military control of the southern operations until he was killed during a B-52 bombing raid in 1967.

PLAF troops would be much better armed and equipped than the local guerrilla units. Many would be equipped with Soviet

7.62mm AK-47 assault rifles, or its Chinese Communist (ChiCom) copies, the Types 56 and 56-1. PLAF main force units would also be equipped with heavy machine guns, in particular, the Soviet SG-43 and SGM, the Soviet DP and DPM light machine gun, and the Recoiless Propelled Grenade launcher (RPG-2). Mortars ranging from 50mm to 82mm were also supplied to these main force units.

The PLAF's most celebrated and prophetic victory took place at Ap Bac on January 2, 1963. It was a set piece battle pitting the ARVN 7 Division against the 261st PLAF Battalion. The battle took place just 30 miles southwest of Saigon in the rice paddies surrounding the crescent shaped villages of Ap Tan Toi and Ap Bac. It was intended as a simple "mop up" operation of a PLAF radio company and its security force. The ARVN, led by General Huynh Van Cao, insisted on attacking with a flourish. Using MP-113 armored vehicles, H-21 Shawnee troop carrying helicopters, and the newly introduced HU-1A (Huey) gun ships, piloted by Americans, the ARVN attacked at dawn.

It was planned that two ARVN battalions would attack from the south, while the MP-113s would roll in from the west. The main

Ap Bac commemorative pins.

attack would then be launched from the north by a battalion of ARVN airborne rangers. Two additional airborne ranger divisions would be held in reserve to cut off any attempt by the Viet Cong to flee to the east.

Everything came apart quickly for the ARVN. The weather delayed landings, and the least experienced units made initial contact with the Viet Cong, quickly being cut to shreds in a deadly cross fire (see map). Attempts to shore up the besieged ARVN elements with additional paratroopers failed miserably when they were dropped directly above the Viet Cong positions and quickly cut to pieces by heavy ground fire from the Viet Cong positions.

When the MP-113s finally arrived on the scene, the Viet Cong burst from their well entrenched positions and attacked them with satchel charges. By 10 PM, the battle was over and the Viet Cong had faded away. They had managed to shoot down five helicopters, including one of the supposedly invincible Hueys. ARVN killed-in-action (KIA) numbered 80, with an additional three American fatalities. The PLAF 261st Battalion would be honored as the "Iron and Steel" squad with special flags, commemorative medals and pins.

In 1963, growing unrest spread across the face of South Vietnam, led primarily by Buddhists, protesting Diem's repression with public immolations, such as that of Buddhist monk Quang Duc, in the streets of Saigon. The U.S. could no longer support the Diem regime. Encouraged by our representatives in Vietnam, ARVN Generals assassinated Diem and his brother Nhu on November 2, 1963. This led to a period of instability in the Republic's government, which lasted until Nguyen Van Thieu (1923-) became President of the Second Republic and Nguyen Cao Ky (1930-) became Prime Minister in June 1965. In many ways, the two, both staunchly anti-communist, oversaw policies every bit as oppressive as those of the Diem regime.

In September 1963, the PLAF instituted a series of formal military orders and decorations (see Chapter 5) to recognize the achievements of its military forces. These orders and decorations generally used the blue and red motif of the NLF flag for their suspension ribbons and bars. Following victory in 1975, and with no longer any need to maintain the pretense of a separate revolutionary movement in the South, eight of these NLF orders and three decorations were adopted as "official" medals of the Socialist Republic of Vietnam. Several other historically significant Viet Cong medals would not achieve this same status.

By 1965, the PLAF, which controlled the burden of the battle in the southern one-third of South Vietnam, had formed its 271st, 272nd, and 273rd Infantry Regiments into the PLAF 9 Division. Later that year, the PLAF 5 Division, commanded by Colonel General Tran Van Tra (1918-), was formed from combined PLAF and PAVN soldiers in the 27th and 275th PLAF Regiments. Its third Division, the 7, was not formed until 1967 and was composed of soldiers from the 141st, 165th, and 209th Infantry Regiments of the PAVN 312 Division. The PLAF's fourth Division, the 1st, was composed of soldiers from the 44th Sapper Battalion and the PAVN 52nd and 101D Infantry Regiments.

Other noteworthy PLAF units included: the 1st, 2nd, and 70th Infantry Regiments; the 1st, 30th, 186th, 261st, 267th, 269th, 501st,

Major General Vo Bam, first commander of the top secret Group 559, which was responsible for the operation of the Truong Son Route (Ho Chi Minh Trail). General Bam's decorations include the nation's second highest medal, the Ho Chi Minh Order. Photo courtesy of Gerry Schooler.

503rd, 504th, 512th, 514th, 516th, D445, D509, 800th, 802nd, 804th, 840th, D857, D7164, Tay Do, U Minh 2, U Minh 10, and Dong Nai Infantry Battalions; the 120th Montagnard Infantry Battalion; the 8th, 52nd, 56th, 58th, and 145th Artillery Battalions; and the 46th Reconnaissance Battalion. PLAF sapper, or special forces, units included; the C-10, 402nd, 407th, and 409th Sapper Battalions; the K-93, V-17, and K-92 Combat Swimmer Companies; and the 8th and H-5 Combat Swimmer Battalions.

Following a series of provocative attacks against American interests in South Vietnam during 1964, encouraged by the Hanoi leadership, culminating in the attack on two U.S. destroyers (Turner Joy and Maddox) in the Gulf of Tonkin, the U.S. Congress passed the Gulf of Tonkin Resolution. It was this act that led to the introduction of U.S. ground forces during 1965 and the shift from an advisory role to the actual prosecution of the war.

With the introduction of U.S. ground forces in 1965, the PLAF's role would be gradually superseded by the PAVN. The PLAF was redirected to concentrate its efforts against ARVN units. This would allow the better trained, more heavily equipped PAVN units to counter U.S. ground forces. The PLAF would continue to prosecute the war in South Vietnam through its major role in the 1968 Tet Offensive. These efforts on the part of the PLAF included a number of significant contacts with American and Australian units during 1966 and 1967.

In August, 1966, the 1st Australian Task Force successfully destroyed combined elements of the PLAF 5 Division, based in the May Tao hills, and the local, full time guerrilla D445 Battalion at the Long Tan Rubber Plantation in Phuoc Tuy Province. The Viet Cong units had been planning an attack on the Australian forward base at Nui Dat. The Viet Cong deployed heavy machine guns (Soviet wheel mounted SGMs) in a ferocious battle that resulted in 245 VC and 17 Australian casualties.

In the fall of 1966 (11/14 to 11/24), the U.S. 1st Division and the 25th Division conducted Operation Attleboro, directed against the PLAF 9 Division, northeast of Tay Ninh, in an area which included parts of the Michelin (Don Dien) Rubber Plantation. Nearly 1,000 Viet Cong were killed in a series of clashes that resulted in the PLAF 9 retreating into Cambodia to recover. The PLAF 7 Division was inserted into the area in place of the battered PLAF 9. The PLAF 9 would remain in Cambodia until early 1967 recovering from its losses.

In early 1967 (1/8 to 1/26), the U.S. Army's 25th Division, augmented by the 196th Brigade, conducted Operation Cedar Falls, again directed at the PLAF 5 Division in the geographic triangle defined by the Thanh Dien Forest, the Hobo Woods, and the Filhol Rubber Plantation. The operation involved the razing of the Village of Ben Suc. Although no single major battle was fought, the Operation resulted in an estimated 750 Viet Cong casualties.

Following close on the heels of Cedar Falls was Operation Junction City (2/22 to 5/14). Junction City involved more than 25,000 U.S. and ARVN troops pitted against then PLAF 9 Division and the 101st PAVN Regiment in a 1,500 square mile area around Tay Ninh. Phase One, which lasted until March 17, involved formation of an inverted horseshoe cordon around the zone. Phase Two involved movement to the east. On March 19 to the 20th, the U.S. 5th Cavalry was engaged in the Battle of Ap Bau Bang II near the village of Bau Bang, astride Route 13. The fierce battle, which pitted Armored Cavalry Assault Vehicles (ACAVs) against PLAF ground forces, resulted in 227 Viet Cong casualties. In all, Operation Junction City accounted for nearly 1,000 Viet Cong casualties. The devastated PLAF 9 was again forced to retreat into Cambodia to recover. It would be smashed one final time at the Battle of Loc Ninh in October, 1967.

During the general uprising, known as the First Tet Offensive, advocated by such leading communist figures as Le Duc Tho (1911-1990), Le Duan (1908-1986), Colonel General Tran Van Tra, and Lieutenant General Tran Do (1922-), the PLAF assumed a major role, attacking villages and towns across South Vietnam, with PAVN forces remaining in reserve. The anticipated "general uprising" of the population against the Saigon government in support of the Viet Cong did not materialize.

Fighting continued for several days with the exception of Saigon and Hue. It took nearly a week to fully restore order in Saigon, following a politically effective (but otherwise suicidal) attack on the U.S. Embassy, the Presidential Palace, and the National Radio Station by 250 main force Viet Cong members of the C-10 Sapper Battalion.

In Hue, South Vietnam's third largest city, two well entrenched NLF regiments, composed of 7,500 PAVN and Viet Cong soldiers, under the field command of Lt. Colonel Nguyen Van and Lieutenant Colonel Nguyen Trong Dan, held out against the U.S. Marine led counterattack for more than a month. Although eventually defeated and forced to retreat, the PLAF had scored a major political and public relations victory by keeping its flag flying over the interior portion of the city, known as the Citadel, during the entire siege. In the aftermath, this important "cultural capital" lay in ruins. It also turned out that the Viet Cong executed scores of civilians (es-

timated between 3,000 and 5,000) deemed loyal to the Saigon government. This massacre received little notice in the generally anti-war press of the era. It was instead overshadowed by events at a little hamlet, known as My Lai.

As a result of severe casualties suffered in the aftermath of the 1968 Tet Offensive, the PLAF would no longer function as an independent, viable military force in South Vietnam. Its role and its remaining units were consolidated under PAVN leadership and staffed by PAVN "fillers." As part of continuing the "independent movement" pretext, the PLAF main force units retained their original Viet Cong designations.

Following the April 30, 1975, fall of Saigon, the PLAF was disbanded, and any remaining cadre were assimilated into the PAVN. Those PLAF units which participated in the May 15, 1975, victory parade held in the newly renamed Ho Chi Minh City (Saigon) marched under the PAVN flag. When questioned about the absence of the Viet Cong flag, PAVN Senior General Van Tien Dung (1917-) replied, "The army has already been unified."

Although the NLF continued to exist until December 1976, when it was merged into the Fatherland Front (its North Vietnamese counterpart), many of its functions had already been replaced by the Provisional Revolutionary Government (PRG), which was formed in June 1969 as a legal counterpart to the government of the Republic of Vietnam. The PRG was headed by Chairman Huynh Tan Phat, a member of the NLF's Central Committee. Vice Chair-

Socialist Republic of Vietnam medal commemorating the Ho Chi Minh Trail operation. The date, May 5, 1961, corresponds with the start of actual infiltration activities on the trail.

men included: Doctor Phung Van Cung, Professor Nguyen Van Kiet and Nguyen Doa.

Madam Nguyen Thi Binh (1927-), who served as a member of the NLF's Central Committee and Vice President of the South Vietnam Women's Union for Liberation, was appointed Minister of Foreign Affairs. The PRG, recognized as the legal government of the South by North Vietnam and several of its Communist Bloc supporters, would represent the southern insurgents at the Paris Peace talks. Madame Binh served as its chief representative in Paris, second only to North Vietnam's Le Duc Tho.

The PRG was granted full recognition at Paris in the agreements signed on January 25, 1973, and became an equal participant along with the government of Nguyen Van Thieu in the National Council for Reconciliation and Concord in South Vietnam.

With the fall of Saigon on April 30, 1975, the PRG soon found itself pushed aside by North Vietnam. In July 1976 Vietnam was unified as the Socialist Republic of Vietnam under the control of the Politburo in Hanoi. The PRG was no longer useful and ceased to exist.

Today, many of the former Viet Cong, with the exception of a number of high ranking Communist Party members such as Vo Van Kiet, who became Premier of the unified country and key member of the Politburo, find themselves once again among Vietnam's disenfranchised. One would need to conclude that the spoils of the Second Indochina War clearly went to the ultimate victors, North Vietnam and the PAVN. On a personal visit to Vietnam in 1993, I encountered many former Viet Cong holding down menial and low paying jobs such as cyclo drivers and museum clerks. There was a definite, but cautious tone of bitterness toward the government in Hanoi. Many complained cautiously of the uneven handed treatment, which they received following the war. Many current commentators are inclined to consider the former members of the Viet Cong as a potential internal resistance movement.

1

VIET CONG GUERRILLAS

The resistance against the French in La Guerre d'Indochine taught the Vietnamese people valuable lessons in conducting a war of attrition. These lessons were put to valuable use by both full and part time guerrilla units operating inside South Vietnam during the Second Indochina War. These units, usually lightly armed and equipped, became extremely effective at raiding small government outposts and communications facilities, rarely conducting any form of large scale or pitched battles. Some major exceptions were the aforementioned Battle of Ap Bac in early 1963 and Operations Cedar Falls (January 1967) and Junction City (February to March 1967). During these encounters, the Viet Cong, to their detriment, entered into large scale battles with U.S. ground forces.

The guerrilla fighter was easily identified by the black pajama uniform and checkered scarf/towel worn by most. Most of the efforts of these units were directed against ARVN forces. During the entire Second Indochina War, the guerrillas continued to maintain a strong presence in the Mekong Delta.

Viet Cong guerrilla uniform.

2

MAIN FORCE VIET CONG

With the infiltration of northern trained southerners along the Ho Chi Minh Trail, the NLF began building a main force army, the PLAF. Armed and equipped by Hanoi and often led by PAVN officers and NCOs, the PLAF bore the brunt of the fighting in South Vietnam through the 1968 Tet Offensive. With the disastrous impact of the Allied Tet counterattack, the PLAF units, for all practical purposes, continued to exist in name only. They would be henceforth staffed and led by PAVN forces.

The main force Viet Cong soldier is characterized by a much more professional military appearance, including uniform shirts and trousers, although wide color variations existed due to wartime shortages. The main force soldier was also more heavily armed and equipped than his guerrilla counterpart. These were professional soldiers with all the accouterments normally associated with such armies. Weapons included heavy and light machine guns, assault rifles, rocket propelled grenade launchers, and a range of mortars. Although the main force PLAF soldiers wore uniforms, for the most part these uniforms were devoid of any insignia. Officers and NCOs were usually identified by the presence of a pistol belt (usually equipped with the ChiCom copy of the Soviet Tokarev (TT-M1933) automatic pistol). Another telltale sign of an officer or NCO was the presence of a ball point pen (often with the English language word "hero" printed on the barrel) in their shirt pocket.

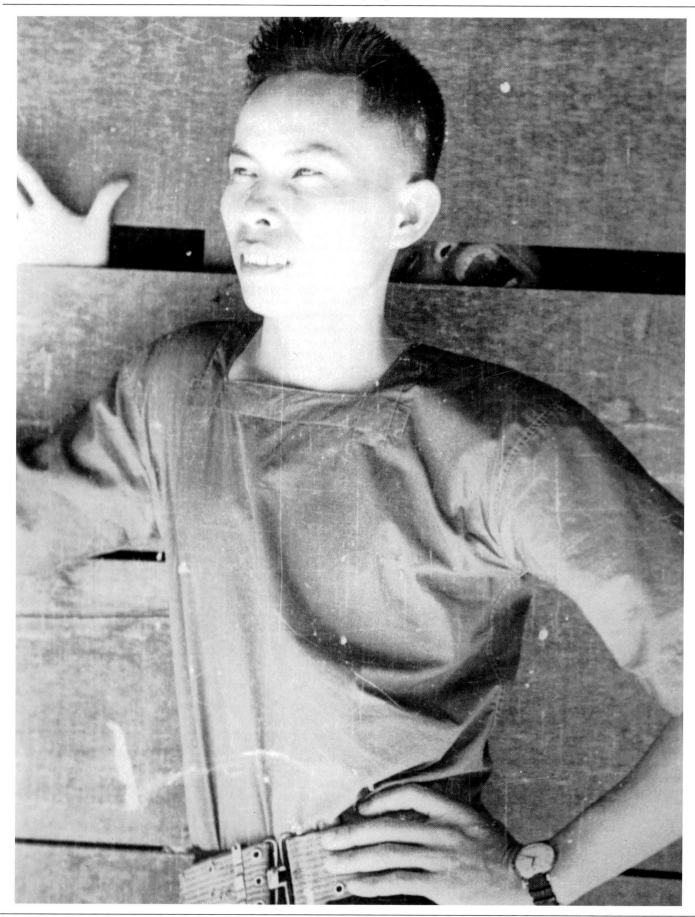

3

VIET CONG POLITICAL GATHERINGS

Like any organization, the NLF held its share of political gatherings, but unlike many organizations, these were generally clandestine meetings held in remote jungle locations. NLF main force cadre were called upon to provide security for these meetings, but there was little defense against sudden U.S. B-52 raids other than hastily dug bomb shelters.

Leading NLF figures such as Nguyen Huu Tho, Madame Nguyen Thi Dinh, Vice Commander of the PLAF, and Ta Thi Kieu, an attractive Viet Cong guerrilla officer and later an international spokeswoman for the NLF, appear repeatedly in these photographs.

To a lesser degree, the Buddhist priest, Thit Thien Hao, and the Catholic priest, Ho Gue Ba, both members of the Central Committee of the NLF, are also observed at such gatherings.

These meetings were held for both organizational and political reasons, as well as for morale purposes. Leading PLAF fighters were often honored as "heroes" (An Hung) or as "soldiers to be emulated" (Chien Si Thi Dua) at such gatherings. In other instances, these meetings were staged to host visiting foreign delegations from NLF supporters, such as Cuba. In one image, photographs of Ho Chi Minh and Fidel Castro are displayed side by side in a visual demonstration of solidarity between Cuba and the Viet Cong.

Viet Cong Hero of the Liberation Army and international spokeswoman Ta Thi Kieu meets Chairman Mao in Bejing.

NLF political badge. *NLF political badge.* *NLF political badge.*

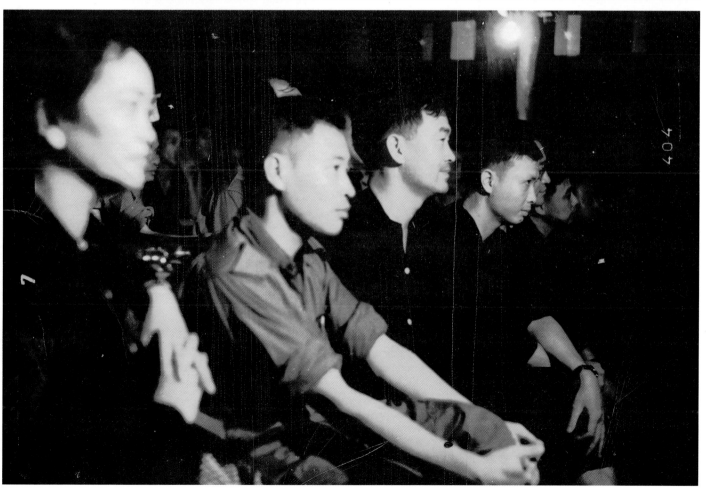

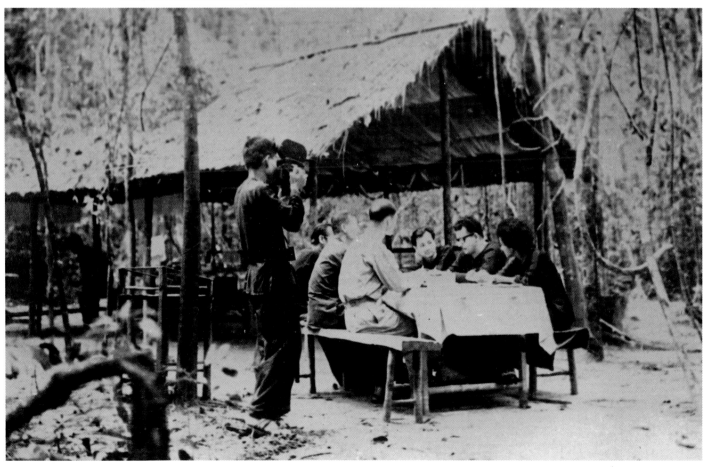

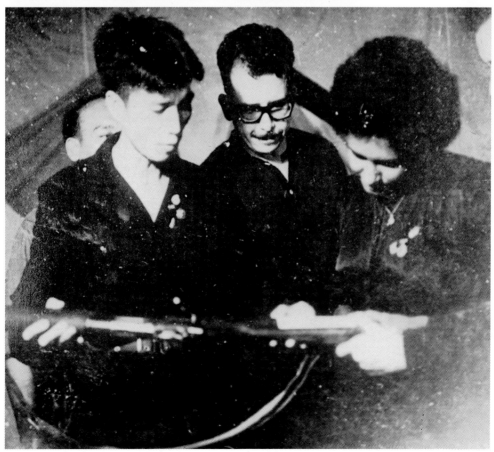

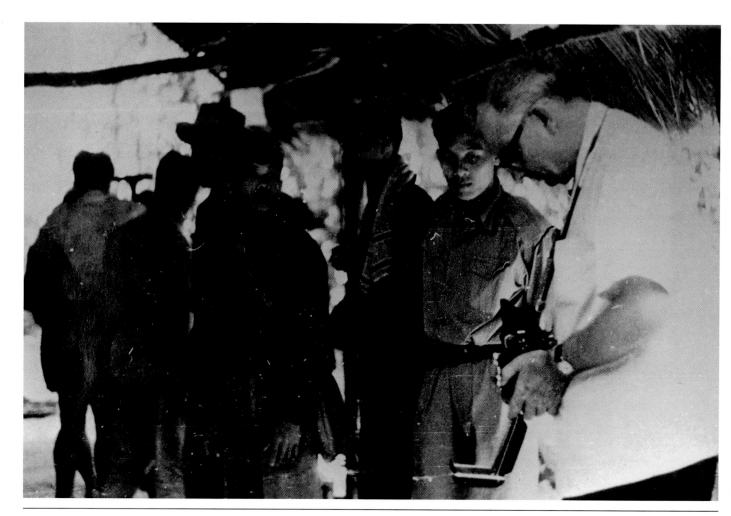

4

VIET CONG WEAPONS

As mentioned earlier, the Viet Cong forces were initially supplied with captured French and WW II weapons to disguise the level of assistance being provided by North Vietnam. Guerrilla forces were generally lightly equipped, consistent with their "hit and run" operations and the fact that, in many instances, they served as only part time soldiers.

With the establishment of the PLAF and infiltration of PAVN soldiers, the quality and quantity of the weapons and field gear improved noticeably. Assault rifles manufactured in the Soviet Union and China, along with rocket launchers, light and heavy machine guns, and heavy mortars found their way south. By 1972, the PAVN had introduced Soviet tanks to the fray in the northern sectors of South Vietnam. Throughout the War, however, both the PLAF and PAVN forces depended heavily on Soviet and ChiCom support and supplies.

Regardless of the level of external support, the Viet Cong did, however, show remarkable ingenuity in the manufacture of local weapons, including guns, mines, grenades, and other forms of booby traps. Many of these unique and deadly weapons were manufactured in crude jungle workshops, making use of captured or unexpended munitions. In other cases, jungle based weavers kept the PLAF forces clothed and equipped with pouches, etc. Chapter 7 features many photographs of these Viet Cong jungle workshops.

Rubber plantation tool used by Viet Cong as an entrenching tool and to clear gun fire lanes in the jungle underbrush.

Traditional formless three pocket back pack.

Homemade pistol.

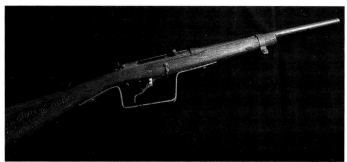

Homemade Viet Cong rifle.

ChiCom stick grenades.

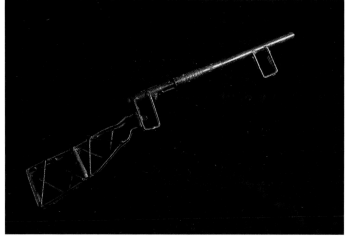

Viet Cong shotgun made from downed aircraft parts.

ChiCom Type 51 copy of the Soviet 8 round 7.62mm Tokarev (TT-M1933) and the ChiCom Type 54 pistol holster with one internal and two external clip pouches. This weapon was carried by Viet Cong main force officers and occasionally NCOs.

Soviet Kalishnakov AK-47 7.62mm assault rifle. This rifle and its ChiCom copies, Types 56 and 56-1, were used primarily by Viet Cong main force units.

5

VIET CONG AWARDS

Starting in September of 1963, the NLF adopted several official orders and decorations based on the Soviet system of pentagonal suspension ribbons for the orders and hero style suspension bars for the decorations. A number of these orders and decorations subsequently were adopted as official orders and decorations of the unified country. Several, however, were not adopted by the unified country, including six unique hero decorations, which were observed being prominently displayed on the right breasts of PLAF soldiers. It is believed the the NLF often awarded bonus payments or pensions based on the number of such hero awards earned.

Prior to 1963, the NLF usually awarded a cloth flower, known as an emulation decoration, to outstanding soldiers based on their military achievements. These cloth flower decorations continued to be displayed even after the adoption of an official medal system in 1963.

Other recognition came in the form of various letters of appreciation or commendation. These certificates, printed on very fragile paper, were often prepared and issued in the field by local commanders. In some cases, they were prepared in the Cambodian Pali script for ethnic Cambodians serving with the Viet Cong.

Another common award, often observed in photographs, was the "hero" pen. These were ballpoint pens, carried in shirt pockets, with the word "hero" printed on the barrel in English.

Seldom worn or encountered Viet Cong cap badges from later (left) and early (right) periods.

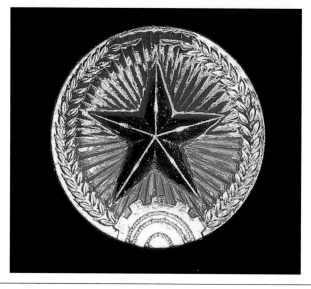

Currently manufactured Viet Cong cap badge made from painting the bottom half of the standard PAVN badge blue.

Hero of the Liberation Armed Forces decoration. Instituted in September 1963, this is the highest Viet Cong combat award.

Liberation Exploit Order 2 cl. instituted in three classes in September, 1963.

Liberation War Exploit Order 1 cl. instituted in three classes in September, 1963.

Soldier of Liberation Order 1 cl. instituted in three classes in July, 1966.

Brass Fortress Order 3 cl. instituted in three classes in September, 1963.   *Liberation Order 3 cl. instituted in three classes in August, 1965.*

Resolution for Victory Order 2 cl. instituted in three classes in August, 1965.

Liberation Decoration.

Resolution for Victory Decoration.

Soldier of Liberation Decoration.

Hero Who Destroys Enemy Communications Decoration.

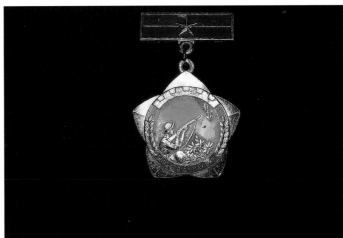

Rare Decoration for Heroes Who Destroy Enemy Aircraft.

Hero Who Assaults the Enemy Decoration.

Hero Who Destroys Enemy Mechanized Vehicles Decoration.

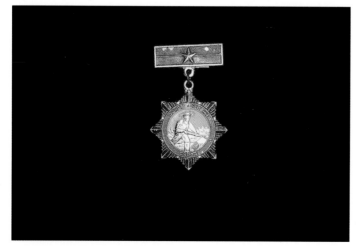

Hero Who Kills Americans Decoration.

Heroes Determined for Victory Decoration.

CỘNG HÒA XÃ HỘI CHỦ NGHĨA VIỆT NAM

Độc lập – Tự do – Hạnh phúc

Số : **602** QP

★

GIẤY CHỨNG NHẬN ĐƯỢC HUY HIỆU

Đồng chí : *Đồng - văn - uống*

Quê quán : *Pleiku*

Đã được tặng Huy hiệu : *Dũng sĩ xung kích*

Ngày *12* tháng *04* năm 19*75*

Universal field issued award document for the Viet Cong Hero Decorations. This particular document is for the Hero Who Assaults Enemy Decoration.

NLF Certificate of Appreciation.

NLF Certificate of Appreciation.

Viet Cong security forces pin, dated 1968.

Viet Cong pin.

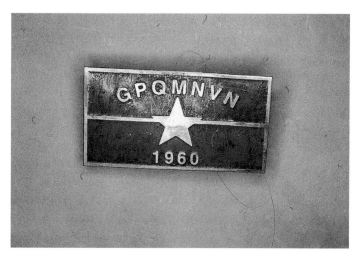

Viet Cong pin, dated 1960.

Viet Cong pin.

Obsolete NLF Liberation Decoration 1 cl. (not adopted by the SRV).

Obsolete NLF Victory Decoration 2 cl. (not adopted by the SRV).

Obsolete NLF Oppose America Save Country Decoration 1 cl. (not adopted by the SRV).

Obsolete PLAF Outstanding Soldier Decoration (not adopted by the SRV).

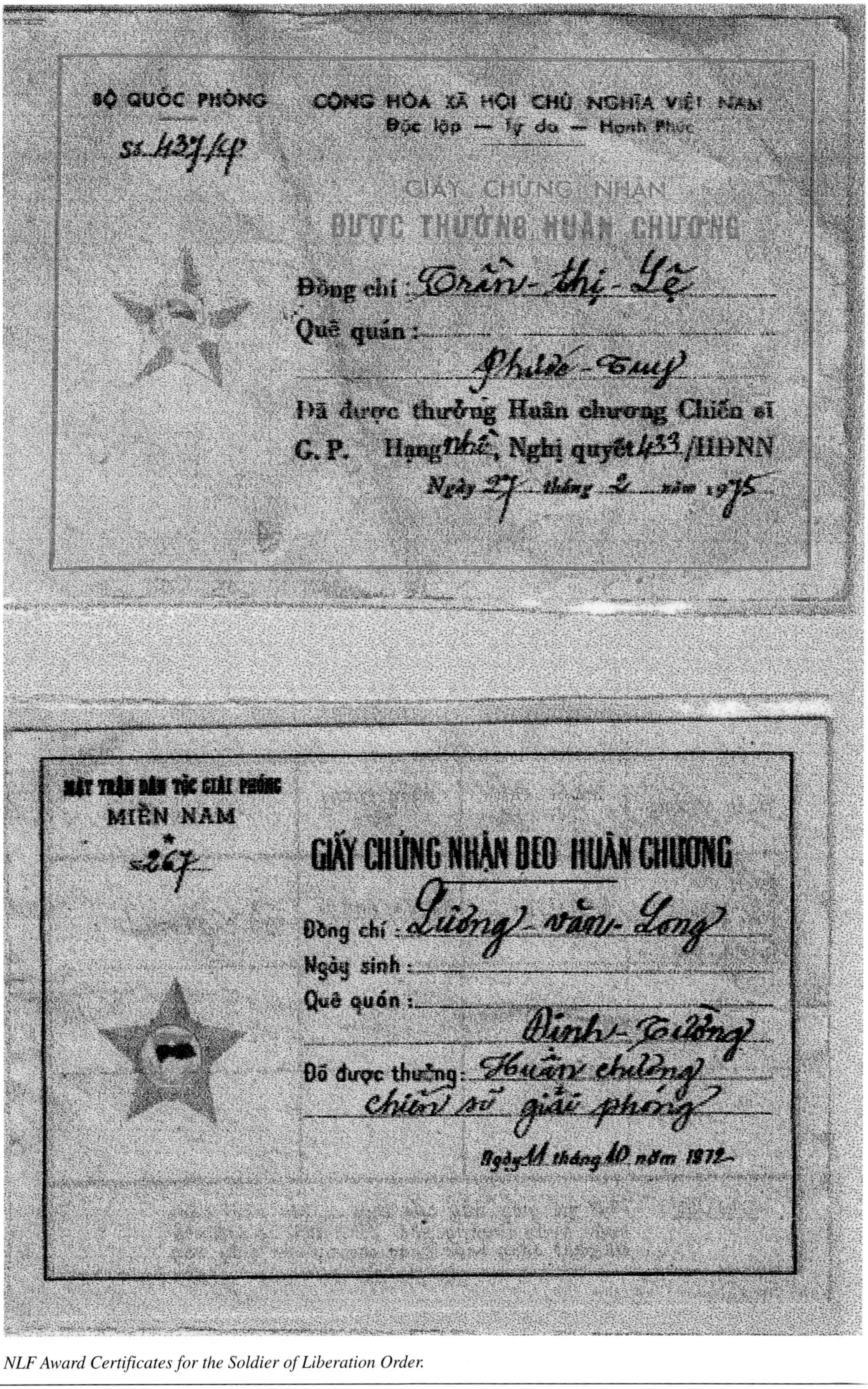

BỘ QUỐC PHÒNG

s: 437/44

CỘNG HÒA XÃ HỘI CHỦ NGHĨA VIỆT NAM
Độc lập — Tự do — Hạnh phúc

GIẤY CHỨNG NHẬN
ĐƯỢC THƯỞNG HUÂN CHƯƠNG

Đồng chí: *Trần thị Lệ*

Quê quán: *Phước-Tuy*

Đã được thưởng Huân chương Chiến sĩ
G. P.   Hạng *nhất*, Nghị quyết *433*/HĐNN

Ngày *27* tháng *2* năm 19*75*

**MẶT TRẬN DÂN TỘC GIẢI PHÓNG
MIỀN NAM**

267

GIẤY CHỨNG NHẬN ĐEO HUÂN CHƯƠNG

Đồng chí: *Dương văn Long*

Ngày sinh:

Quê quán:
Bình Tường

Đã được thưởng: *Huân chương
chiến sĩ giải phóng*

Ngày *11* tháng *10* năm 19*72*

NLF Award Certificates for the Soldier of Liberation Order.

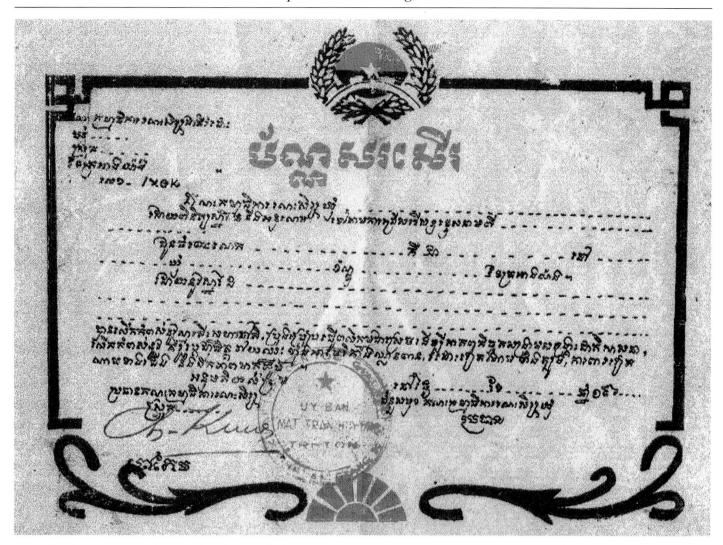

Cambodian language award document for ethnic Cambodians serving in the Viet Cong.

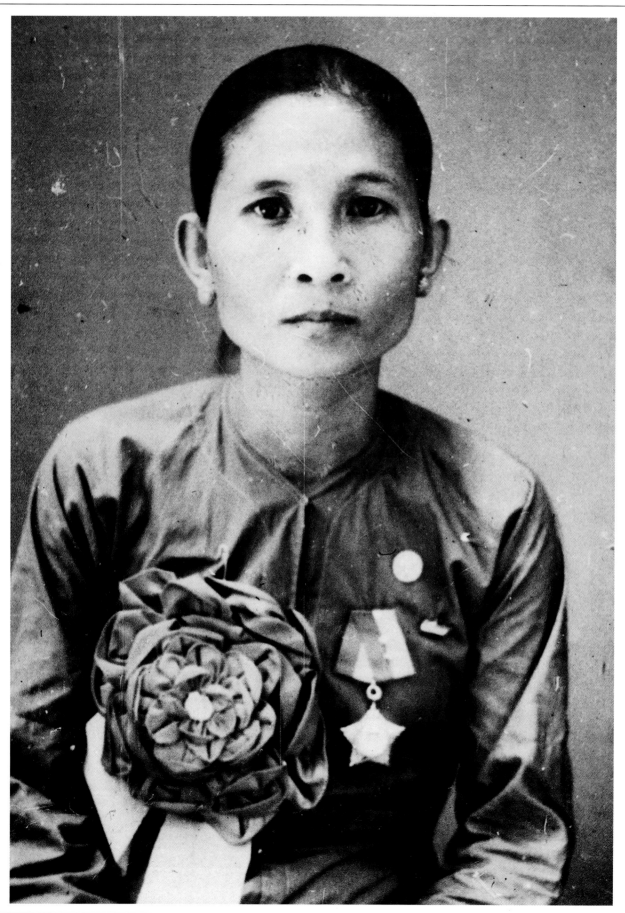

6

VIET CONG ARTISTIC TROUPES

Entertainment of the troops in the field had as much priority for the PLAF as it did for the Allied forces. Traveling minstrel, dance, and acting troupes were a large part of Viet Cong life in the jungle. These troupes often performed highly political music or plays, geared toward enforcing the Communist Party's propaganda message and encouraging the Viet Cong forces to strive for victory.

Some commentators suggest that such entertainment may have also extended to traveling brothels. Reference is made to a secret Ho Ly, or Satisfaction Support Unit, organized for the sexual benefit of high ranking PLAF officers. This practice was introduced into the region by the French Colonial Forces, but it is unlikely that the puritanical and austere PAVN leaders would have endorsed such practices, especially as they began assuming a greater role in the struggle in the mid to late 60s. Certainly staunch Communist Party members would have never condoned the existence of such a unit.

The efforts of these entertainers and the rigors they experienced in the jungle were commemorated by at least two "unofficial" medals, one which was known as the Cultural Soldier medal, and the other which was locally issued in Ho Chi Minh City (Thanh Pho Ho Chi Minh).

Cultural Soldier Medal.

Artistic Troupe Medal.

7

VIET CONG JUNGLE LIFE

If the topic of jungle life could be summed up in a single word, it would be "harsh." The PLAF and the guerrilla fighters spent vast amounts of time in some of the most inhospitable areas on the planet. They were exposed to harsh weather conditions, including monsoon rains, poisonous snakes and insects, and equally dangerous germs and bacteria.

To overcome the demoralizing effects of these conditions, often coupled with inadequate food supplies, PLAF commanders adhered to a strict regime of daily life on the theory that a busy soldier would have little time to become demoralized. Work details were carefully organized and strict work schedules were enforced. Local support troops acted as cooks, weavers, munitions makers and gun smiths. The typical work schedule extended (depending on the amount of daylight) for up to 19 hours, with only brief rest periods allowed for meals. During a typical non-operational day, time was allocated to both military training as well as political indoctrination.

Camp discipline was maintained through a system of self criticism. Only the most serious crimes received harsher treatment, including expulsion from the Communist Party.

Because of the shortage of draft age candidates available to the PLAF, women and ethnic minorities were heavily recruited. Although with the minor exception of an all female guerrilla combat unit operating in Bentre Province, most women were relegated to support roles. Cambodian and Montagnard males, however, played significant combat roles in the Viet Cong. The Montagnard Viet Cong officer, Bi Nang Thak of the Raglay Tribe, achieved the lofty status of "Hero of the Liberation Armed Forces."

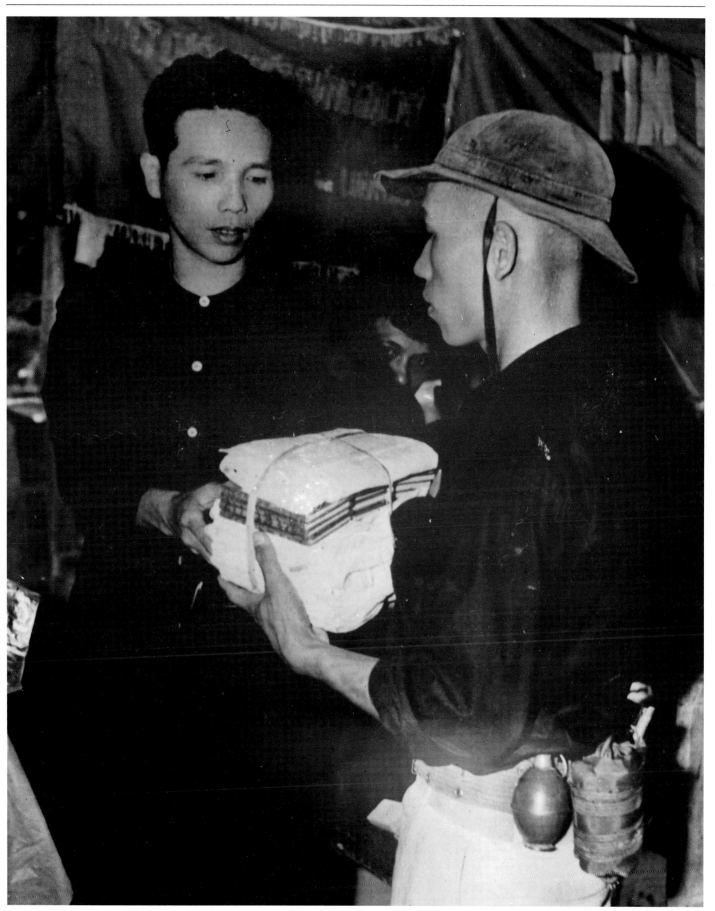

BIBLIOGRAPHY

Conboy, Ken, Bowra, Ken and McCouaig, Simon: *The NVA and Viet Cong*. London: Osprey Publishing, Ltd., 1991.

Emering, Edward: *NVA/VC Weapons and Field Gear*. Atglen, PA: Schiffer Publishing, Ltd., 1998.

Emering, Edward: *Orders Decorations and Badges of the Socialist Republic of Vietnam*. Atglen, PA: Schiffer Publishing Ltd., 1996.

Kutler, Stanley: *Encyclopedia of the Vietnam War*. New York: MacMillan Library Reference, 1996.

Lanning, Michael Lee and Cragg, Dan: *Inside the VC and the NVA*. New York: Fawcett Columbine, 1992.

Moyer, Mark: *Phoenix and The Birds of Prey*. Annapolis, Maryland: Naval Institute Press, 1997.

Pike, Douglas: *People's Army of Vietnam*. New York: Da Capo Press, 1996.

Truong Nhu Tang: *A Viet Cong Memoir*. New York: Vantage Books, 1986.